AWESOME ANIMALS
Coloring Book

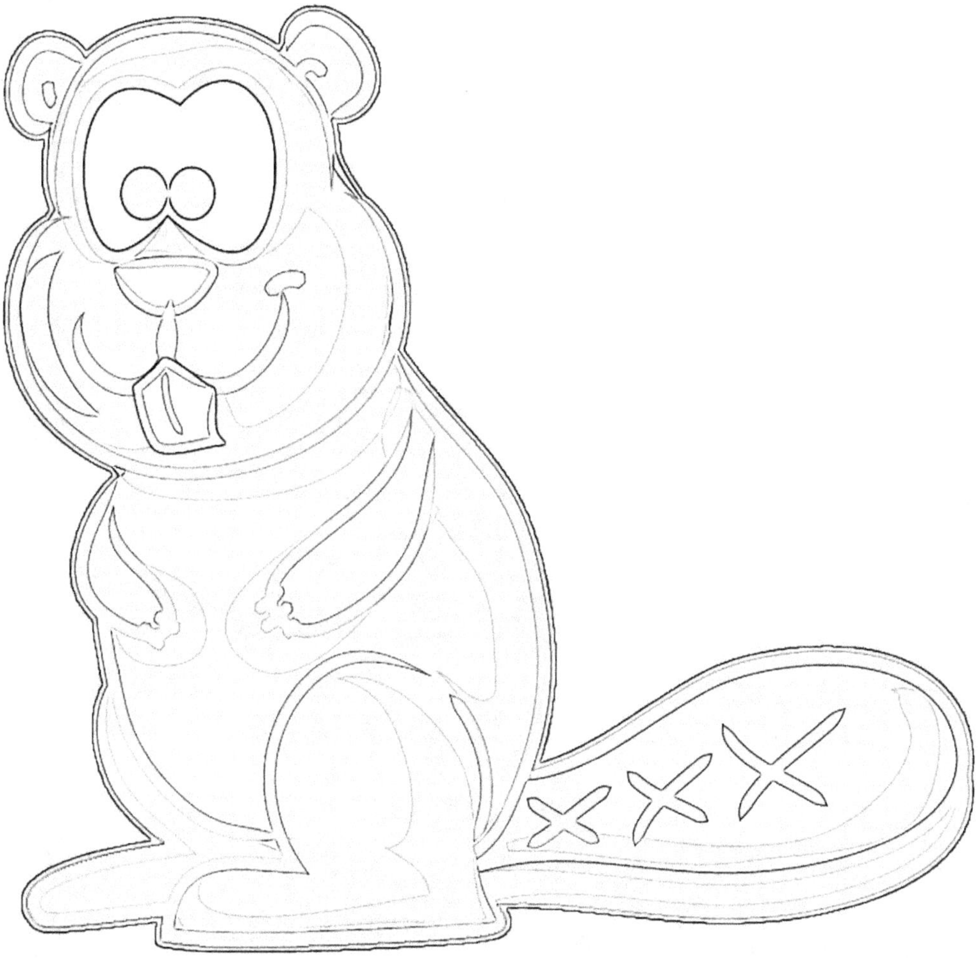

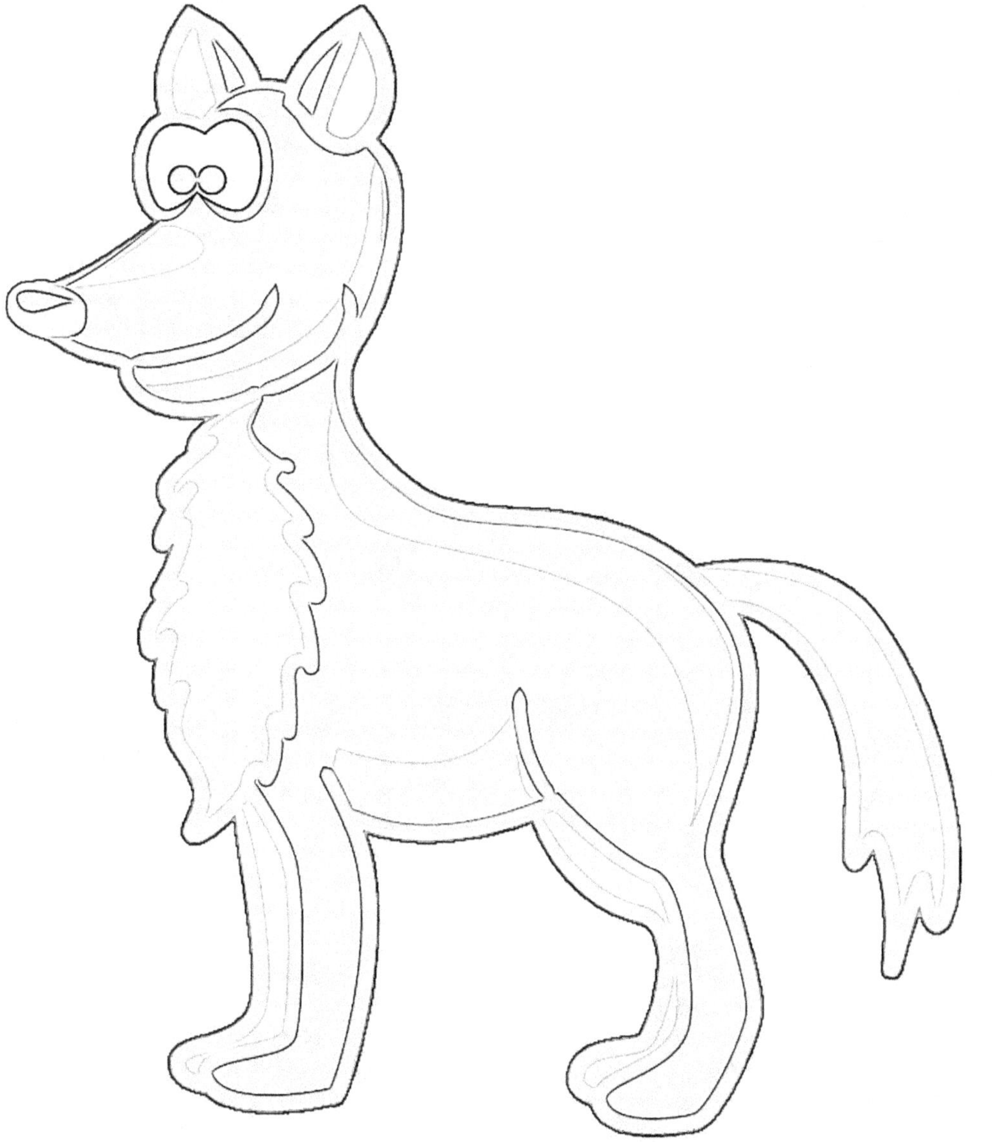

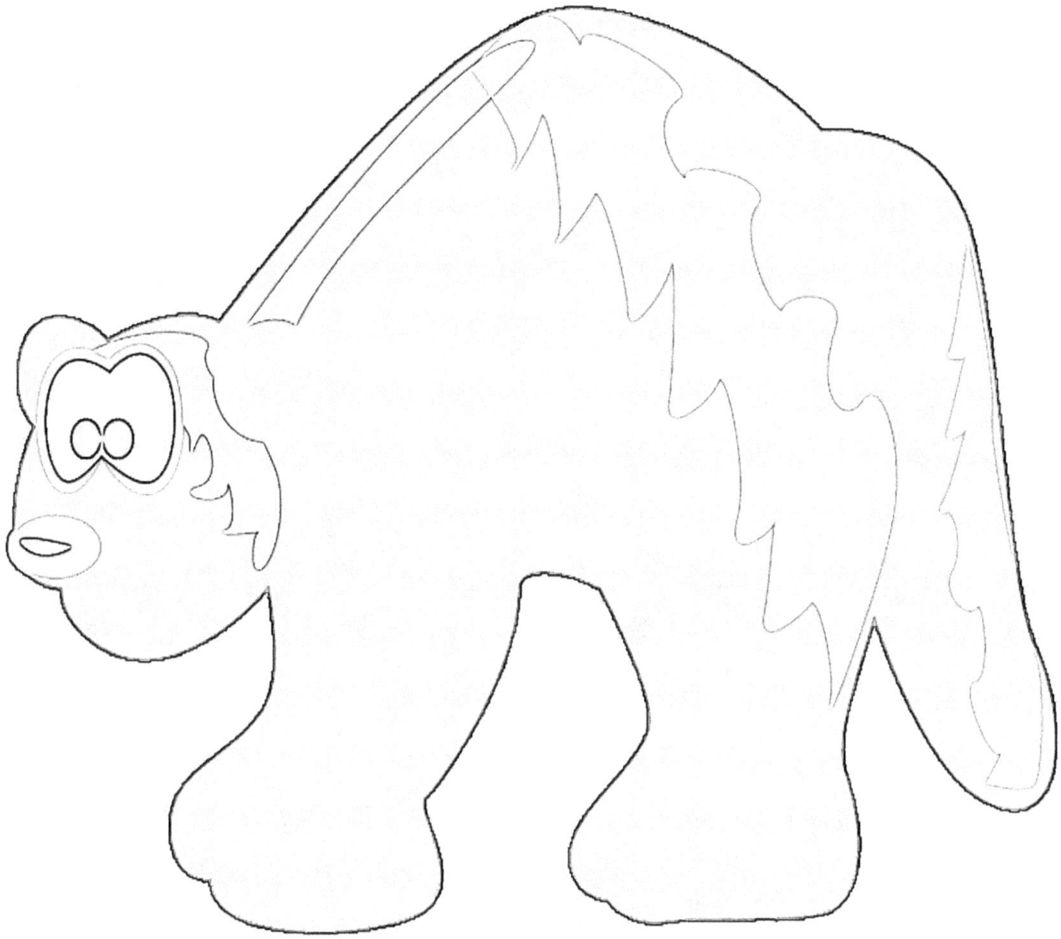

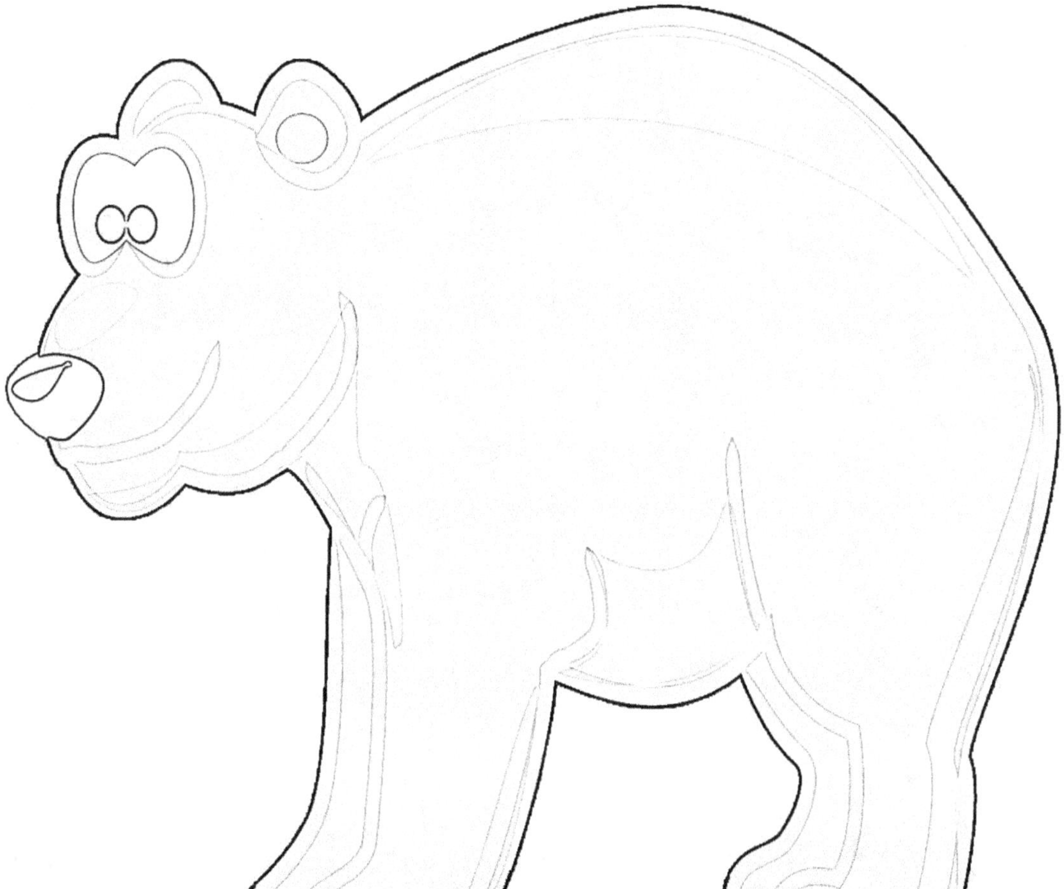

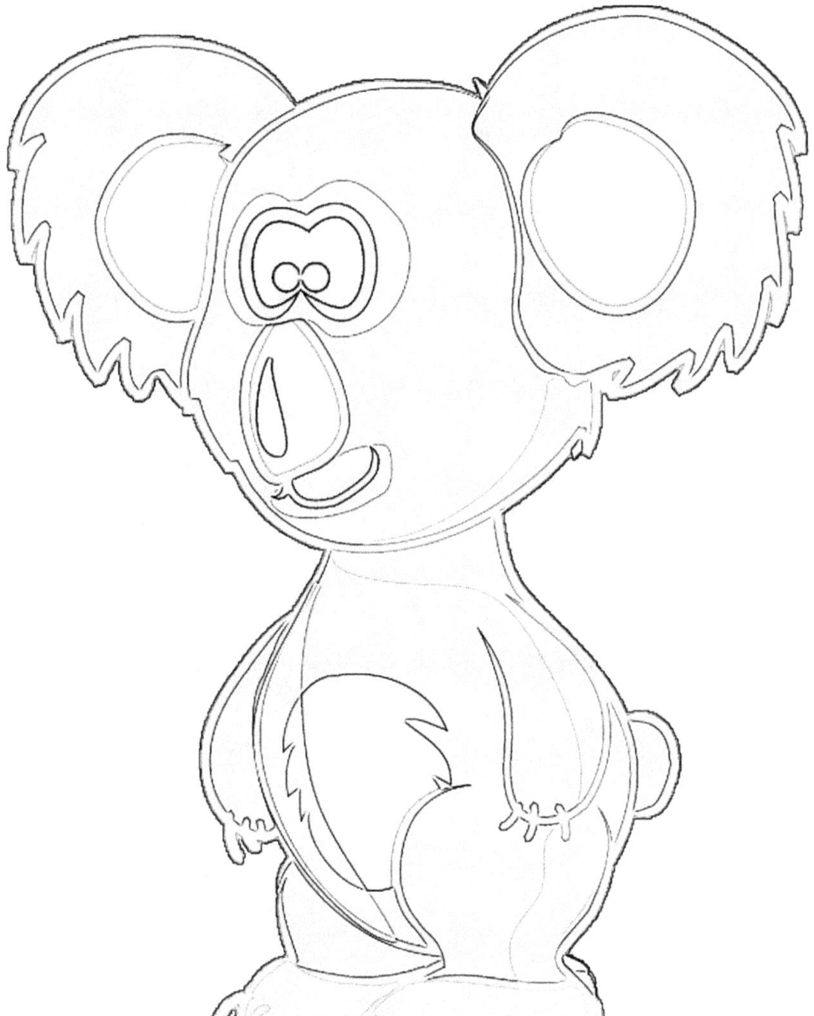

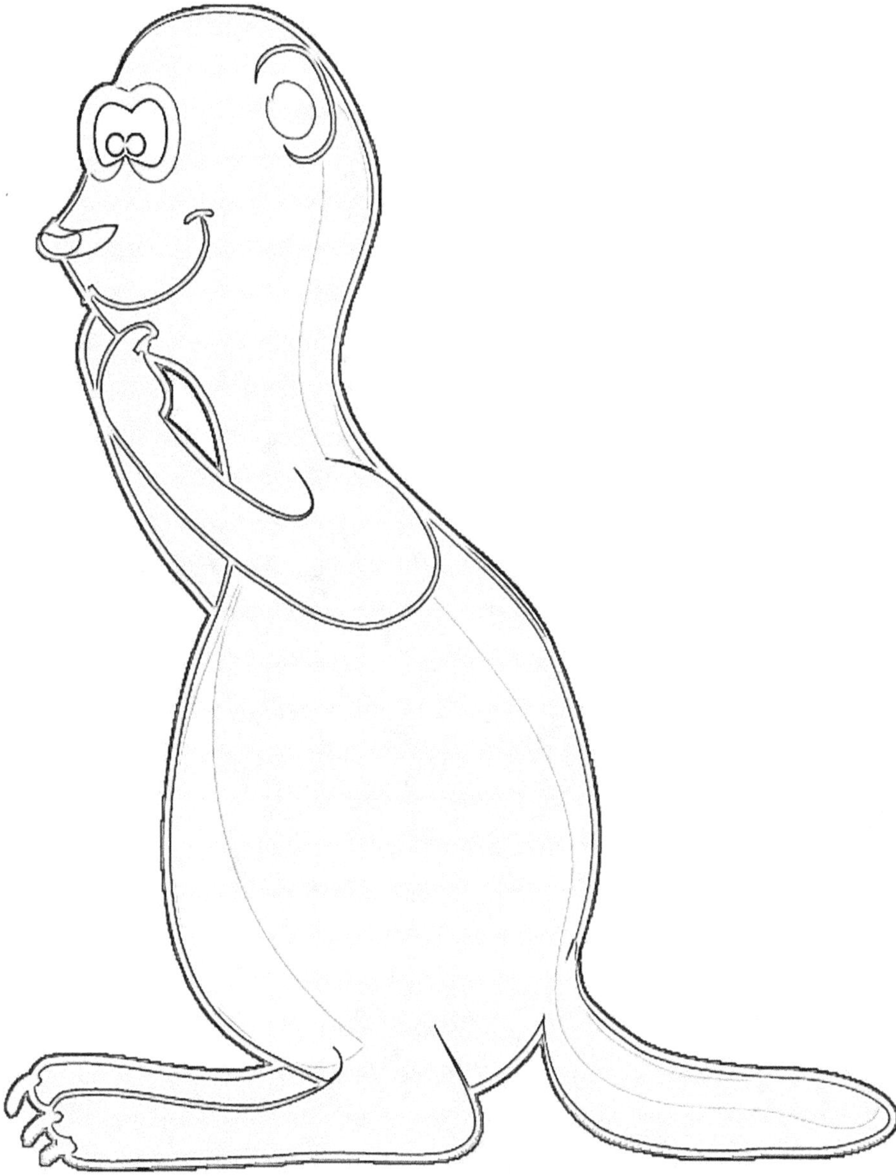

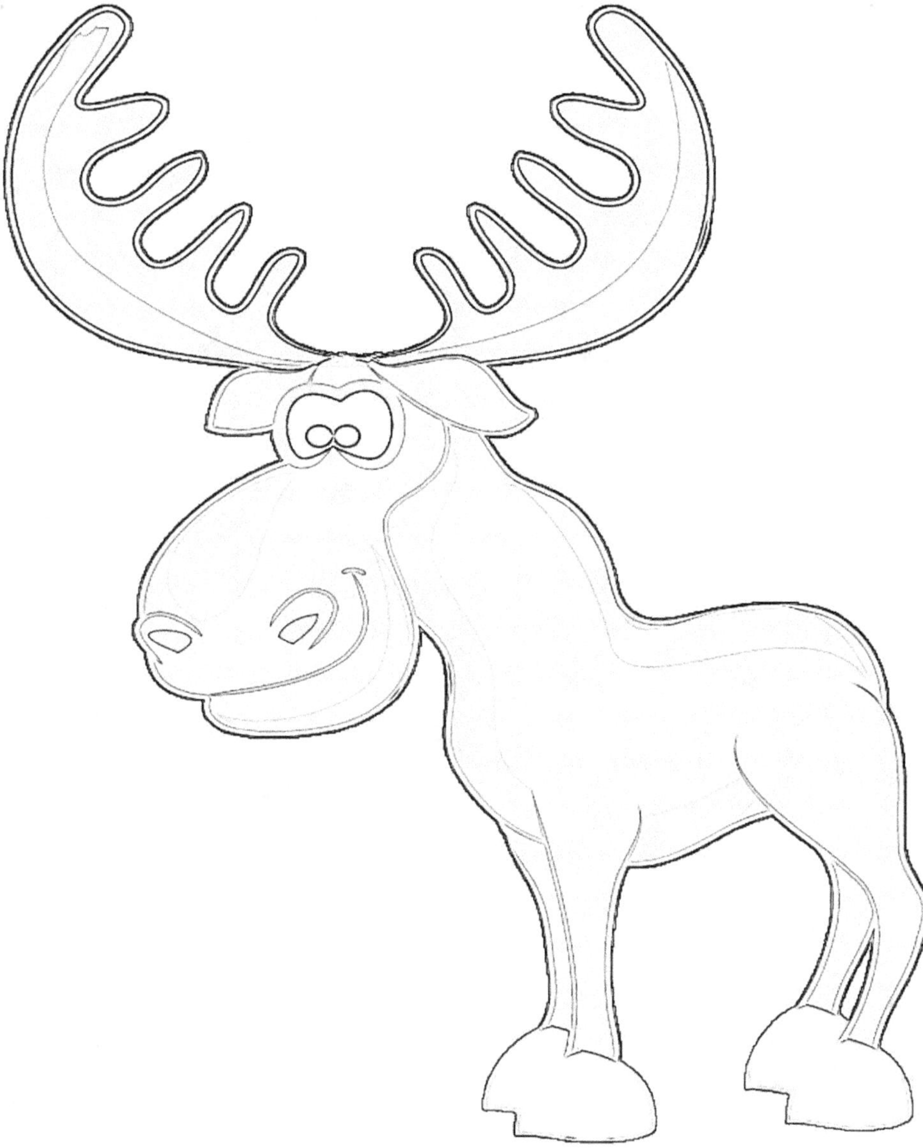

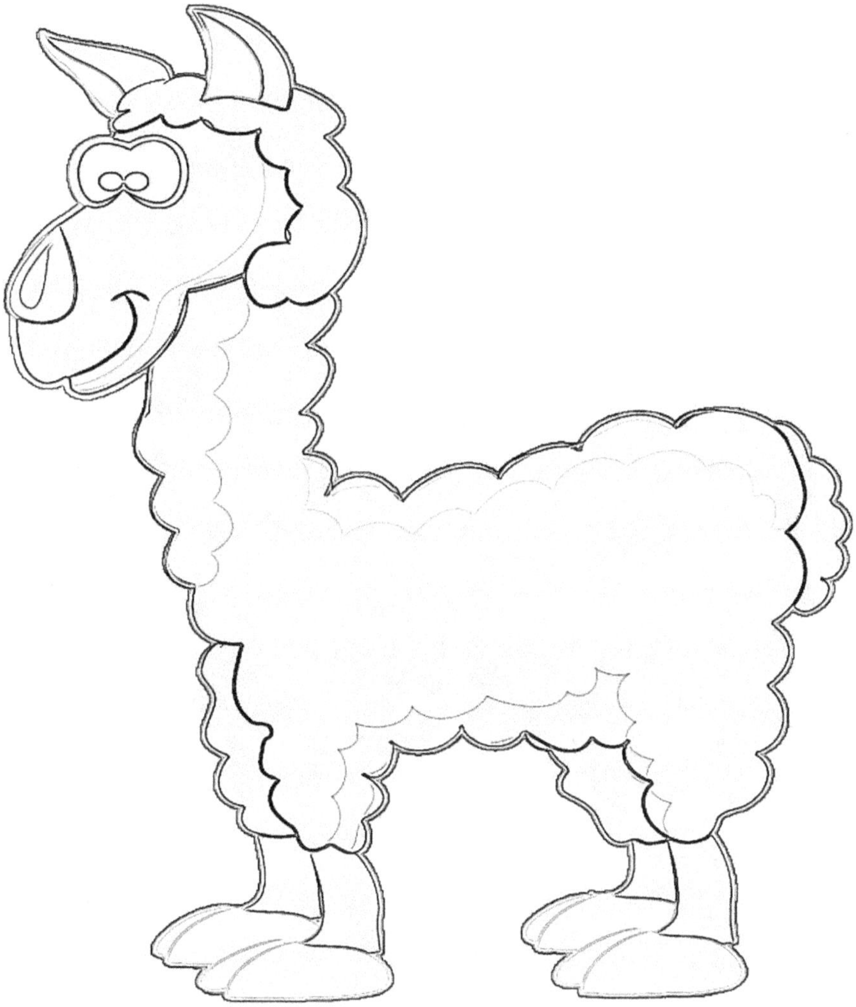

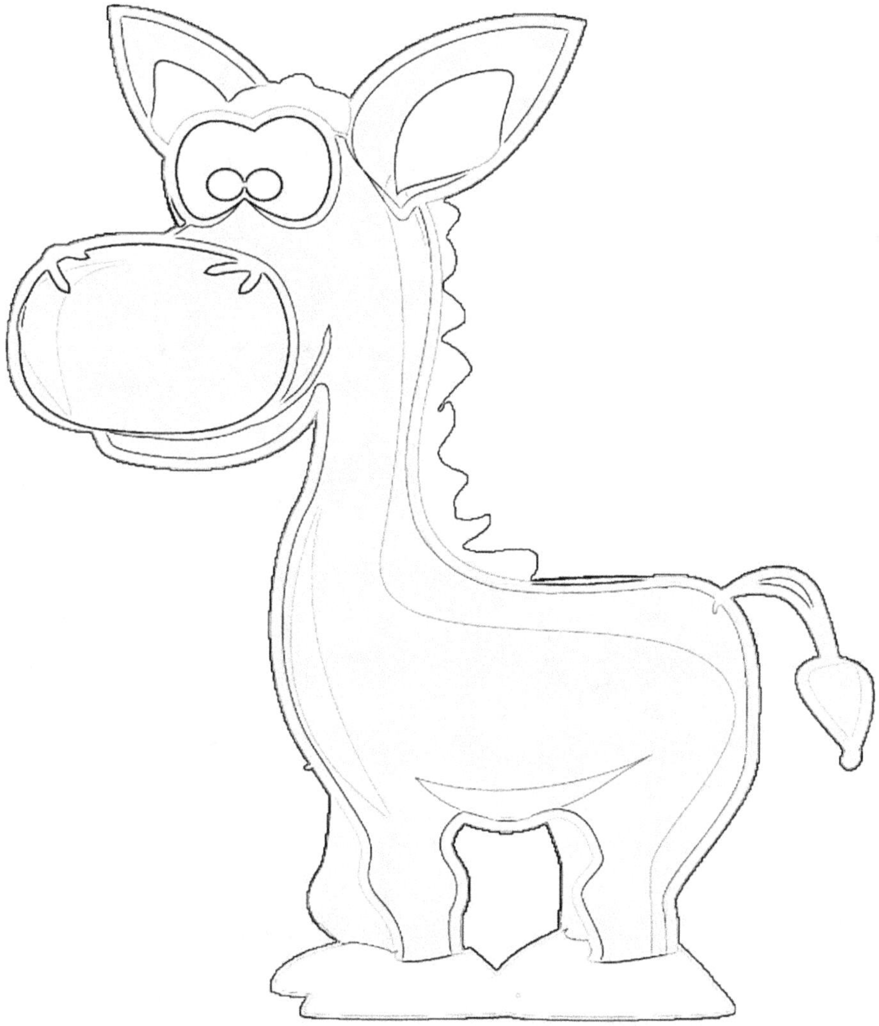

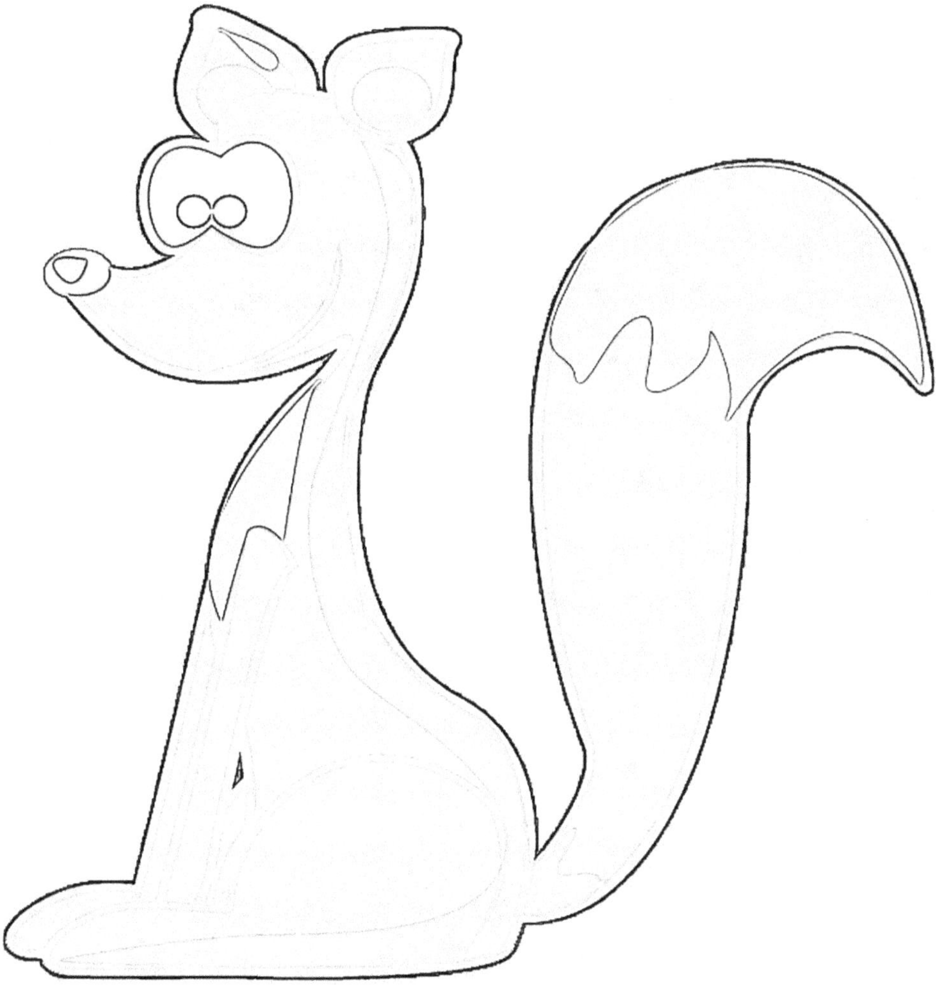

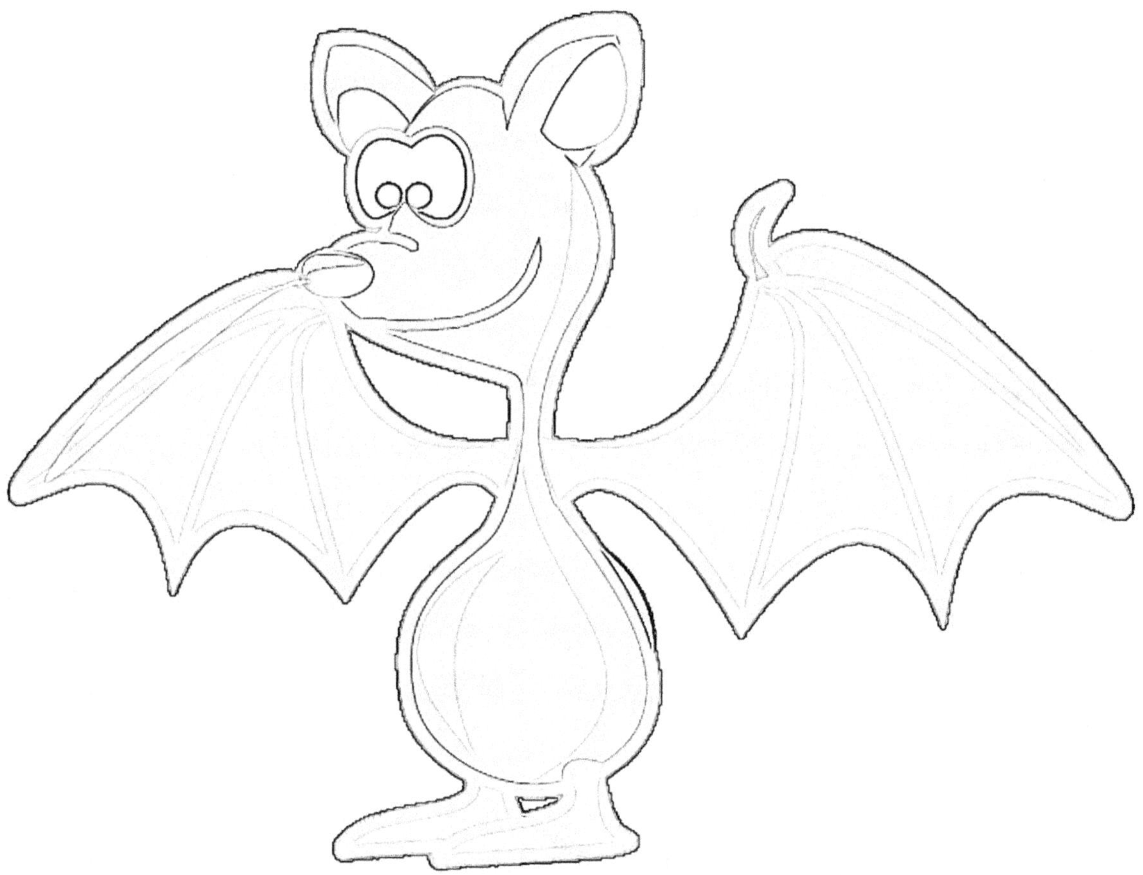

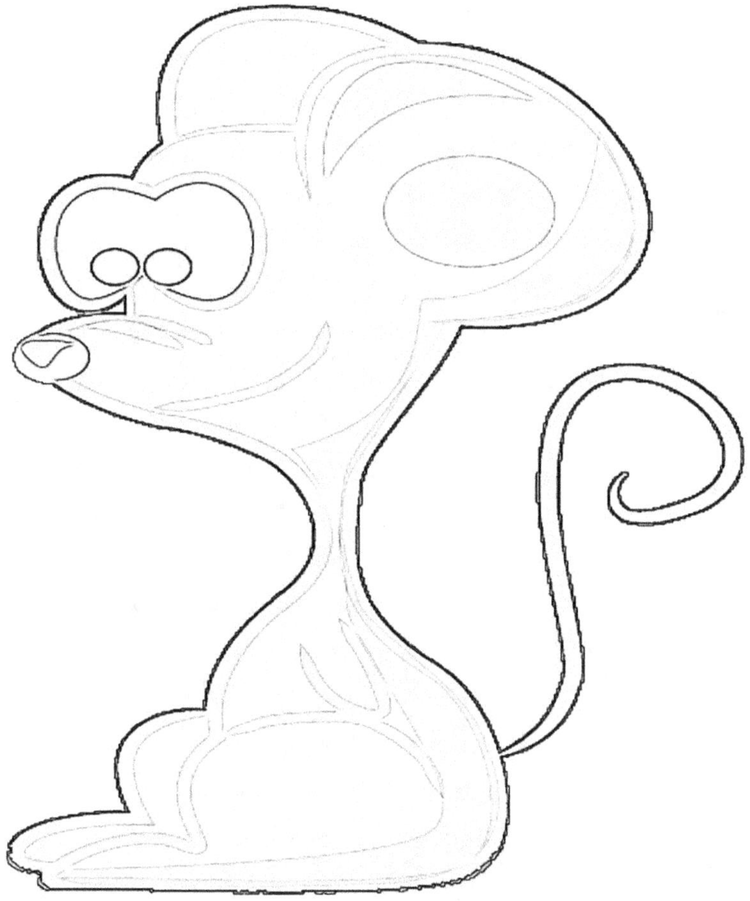

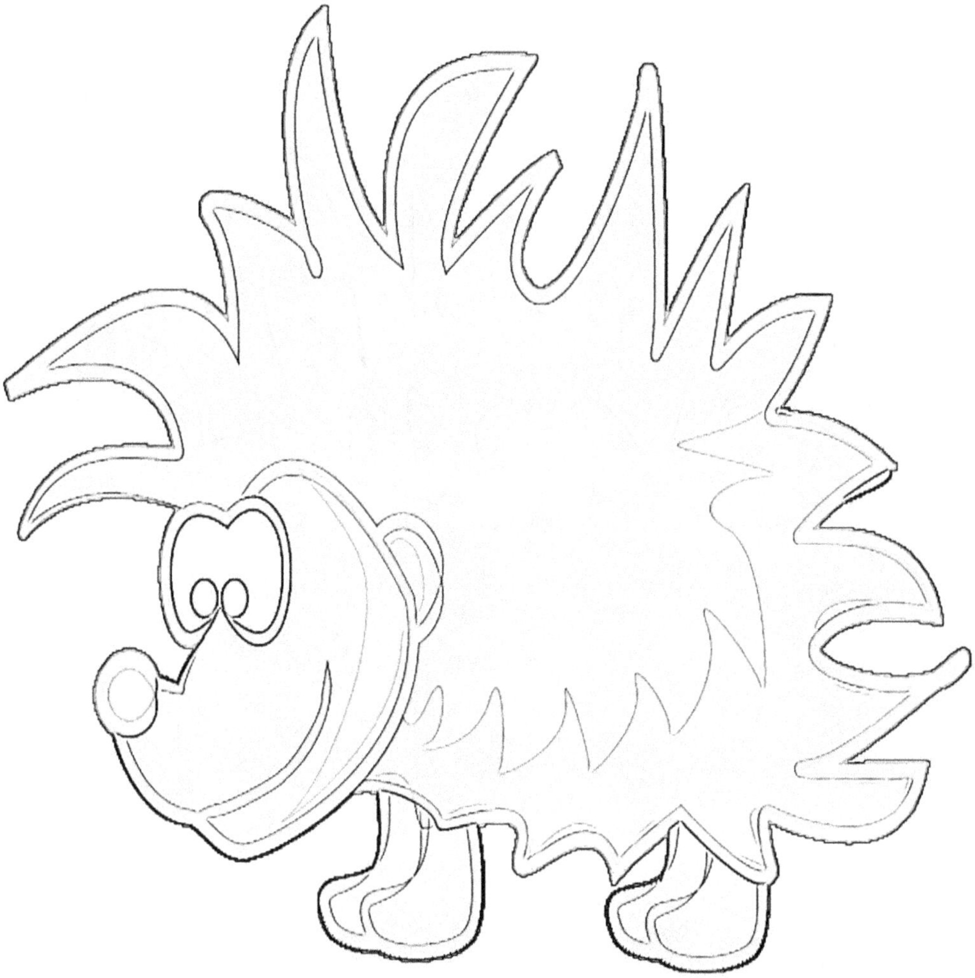

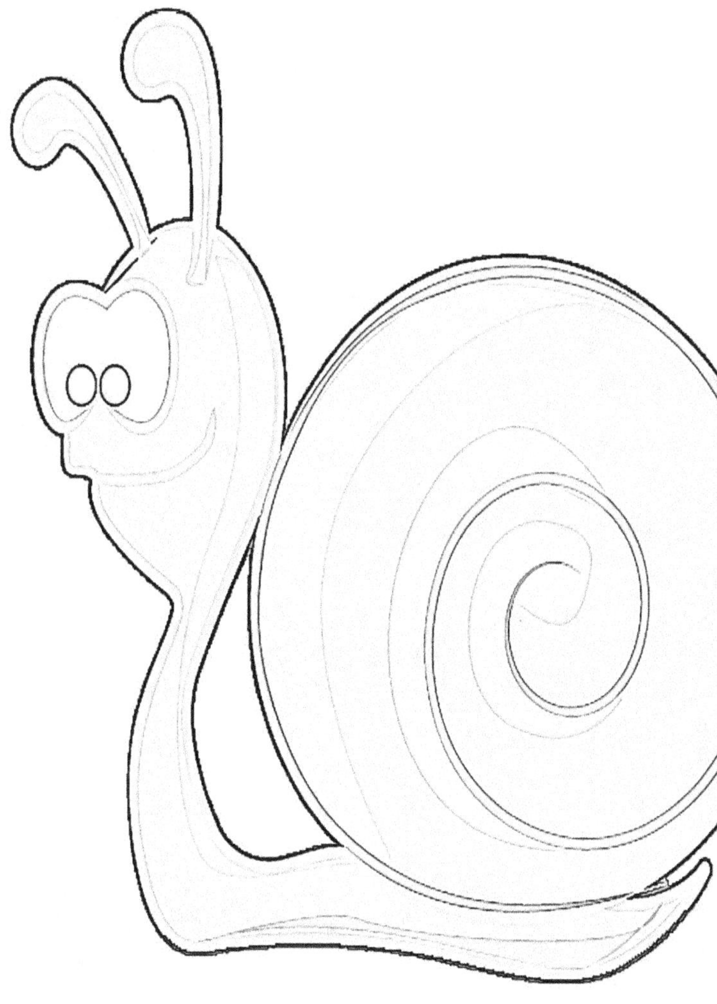

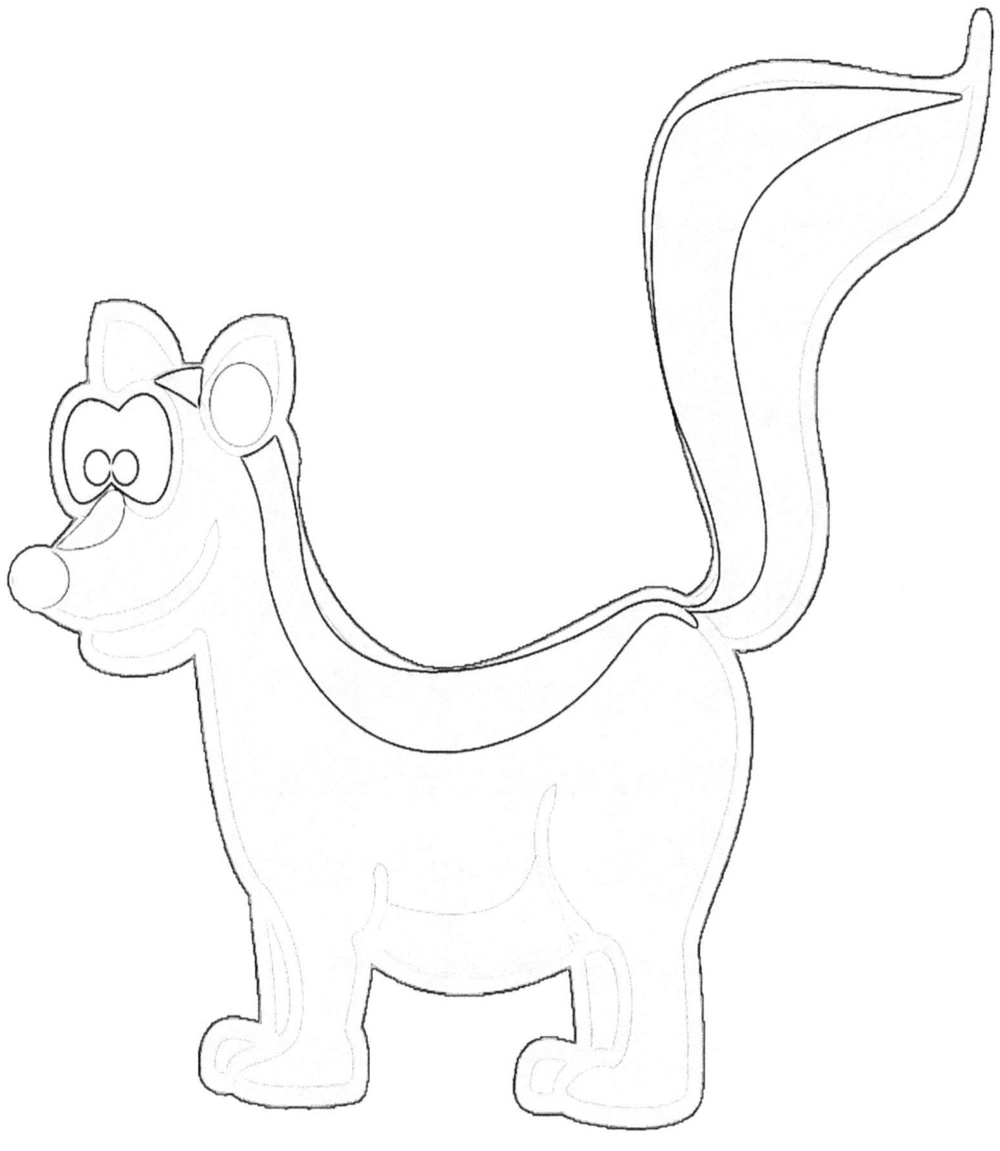

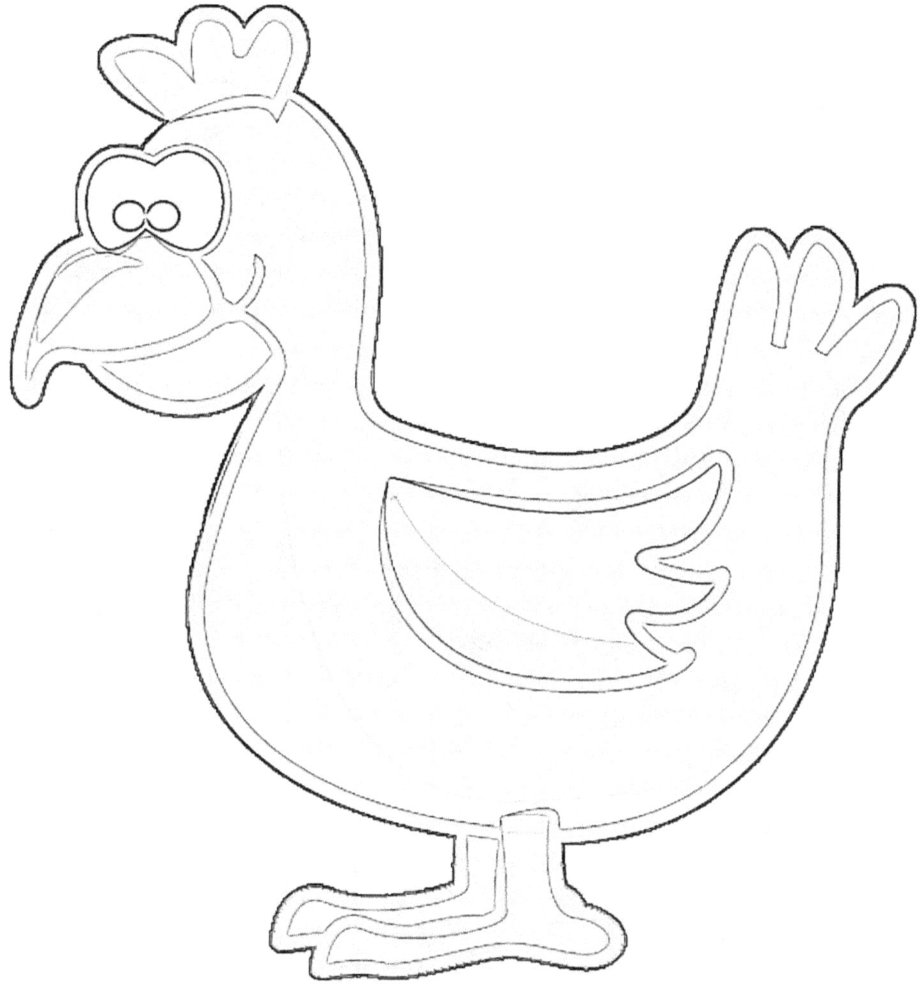

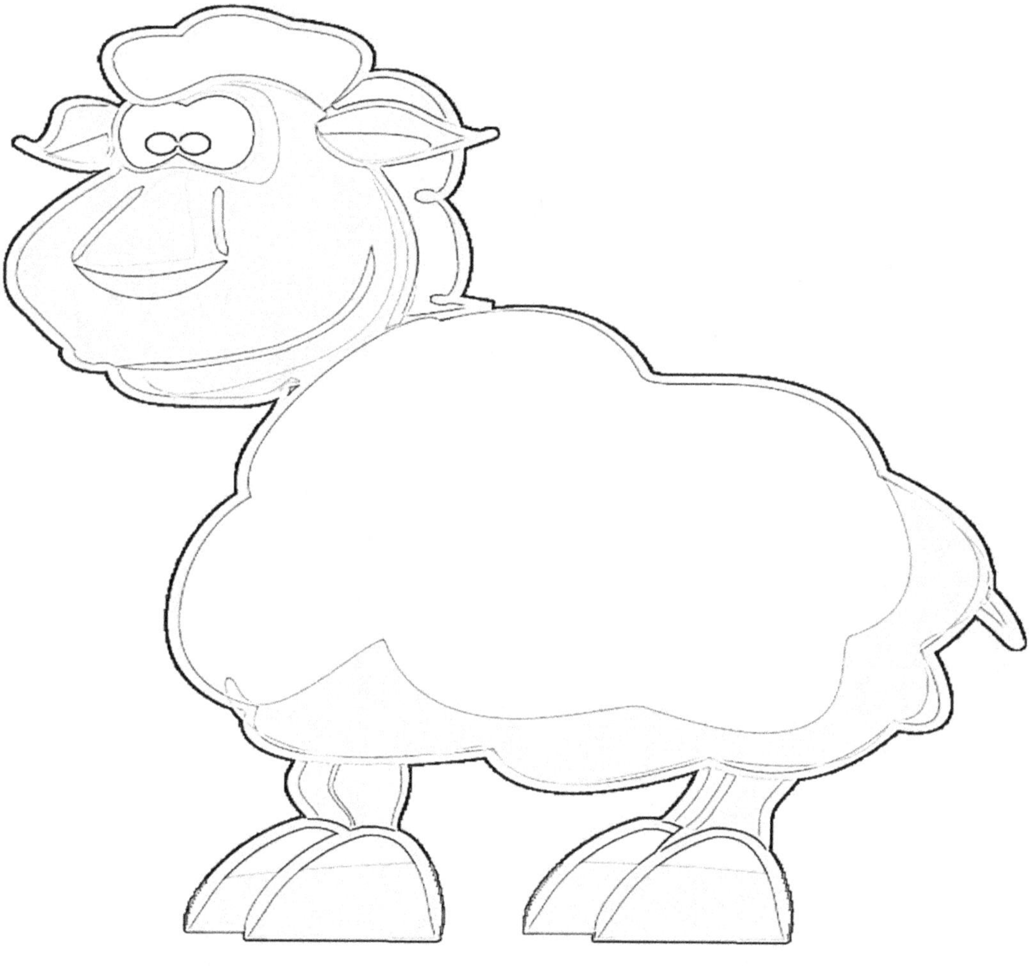

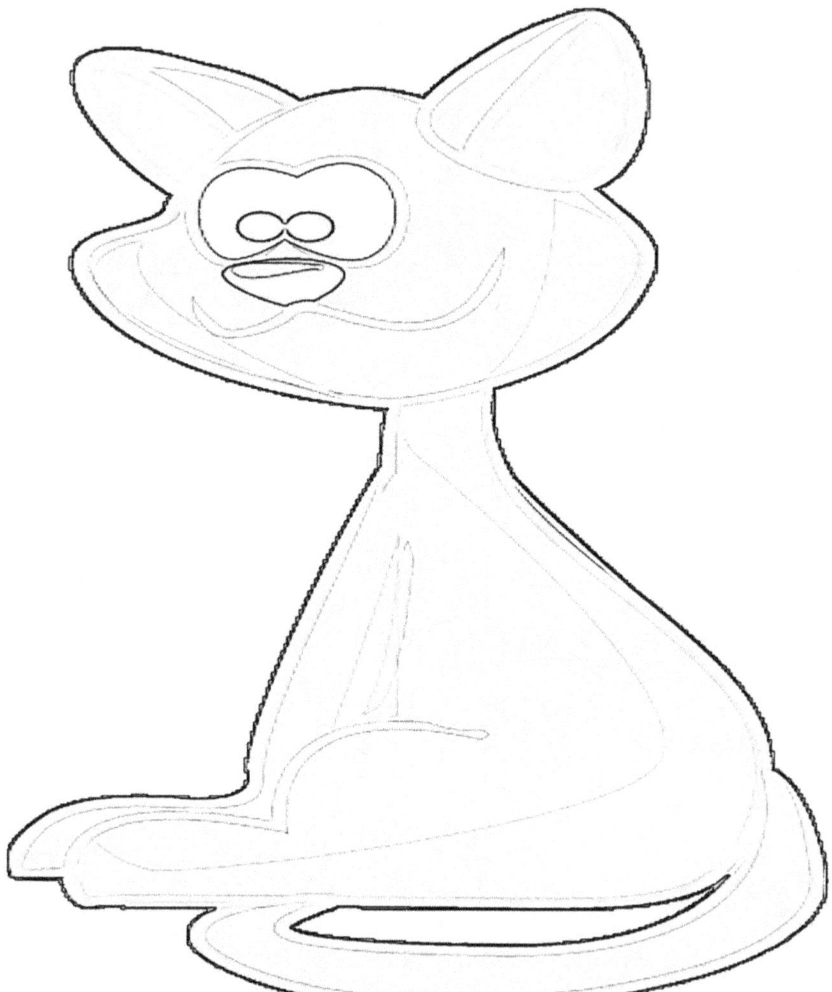

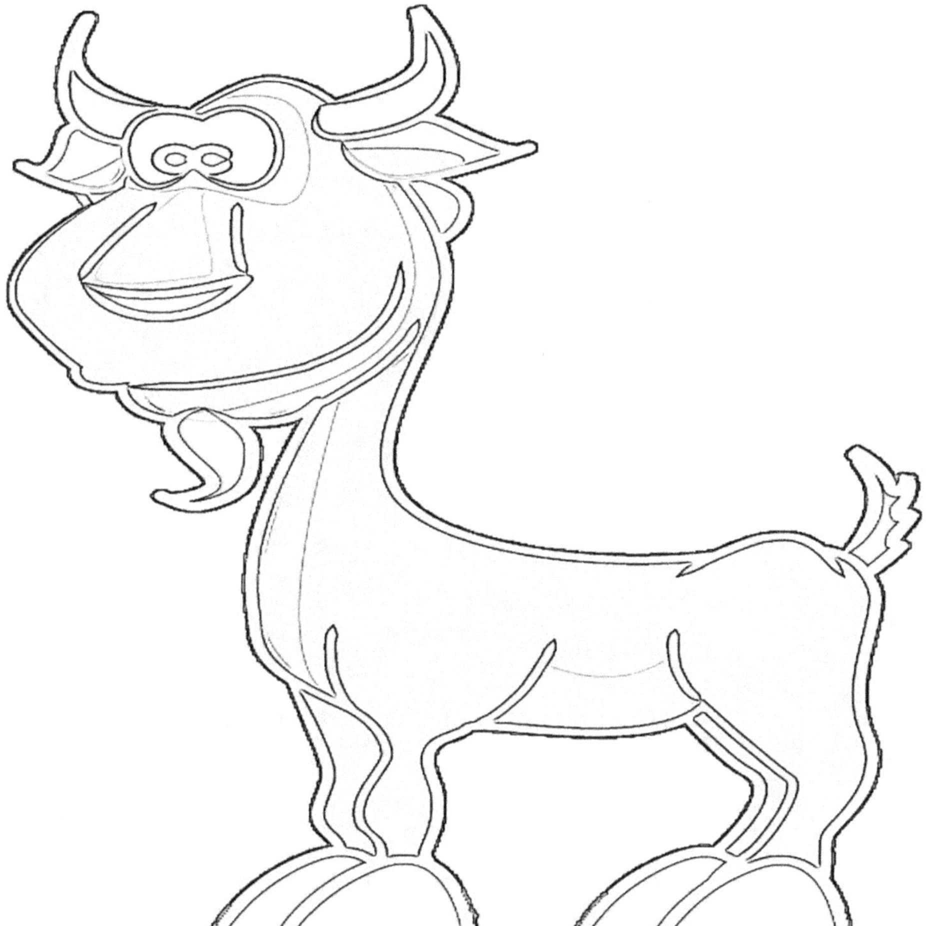

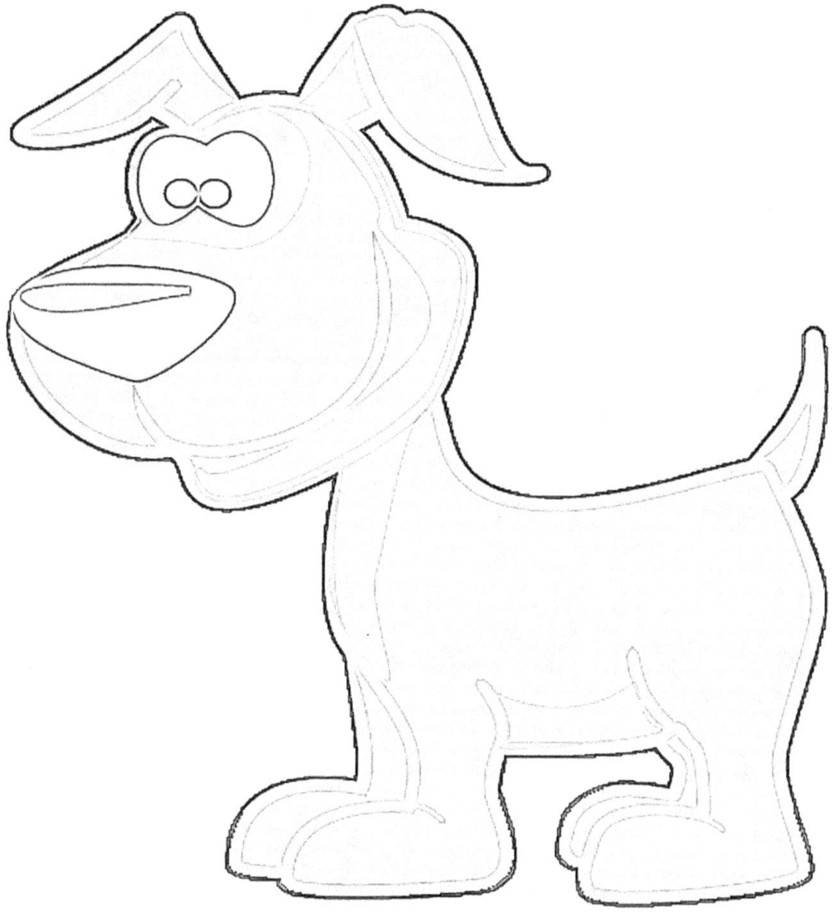

www.ingramcontent.com/pod-product-compliance
Lightning Source LLC
Chambersburg PA
CBHW081401170526
45166CB00010B/3159
* 9 7 8 1 5 1 9 4 0 9 9 1 1 *